4 99

# Turning the Tide

*by*

## Malcolm Smith

Albury Press
2448 East Lewis Street, Suite 4700
Tulsa, Oklahoma 74137

*Turning the Tide*
ISBN 1-88008-925-4
Copyright © 1995 by Malcolm Smith
Malcolm Smith Ministries
P. O. Box 29747
San Antonio, TX 78229-0747

Published by: **Albury Press**
2448 East Lewis Street, Suite 4700
Tulsa, Oklahoma 74137

Editor: Jan Oualline

# Table of Contents

# Preface

A few years ago, we watched the city of Los Angeles erupt into a war zone of hate. Innocent people were savagely beaten before our eyes, and lifetimes of work were lost within a few hours during the senseless burning of entire neighborhoods.

Every evening as we sit and watch the evening news, reports of rape, murder, and robbery fill the television screen, even in small rural communities. But in our large cities, there seems to be a total loss of control when it comes to dealing with crime.

The concept of family is being redefined whether we like it or not. Children are now being raised by homosexual or lesbian lovers — readily accepted as "alternate lifestyles" — and the idea of a mother, father, and children who live together in the same house, eat together, play together, love together, and talk together has almost disappeared from all forms of media entertainment.

When you consider the number of hours both children and adults in America spend being instructed by their television sets, VCRs, and movie screens, you can easily understand why our people are so easily lulled into the acceptance of violence, indiscriminate sex, and a complete redefinition of the family.

The sacredness of life is cheapened on our streets by violence that defies imagination, and yet street gangs, who have no concept of human life having any value, have also become a new "family" of the 90s. According to a 1993 Barna Research Group study, in Los Angeles, gang members outnumber police by ten to one. By the year 2000, gangs will be a nationwide reality, not just found in the large cities.

Sex education in the schools has taken all meaning out of sex. It is simply mechanical pleasure that is enjoyed by humans, and this can be with as many humans as can be fit into one day. It has no more meaning than eating breakfast. Condoms are given to ten- and eleven-year-olds because it is assumed they will be trying it out.

More value is placed on the lives of animals than on humans. We protect animals and their environment while allowing and endorsing the mutilation and death of thousands of human babies each year through abortion. They are either in the way or could be an embarrassment.

If our children are allowed to be born, you will find many reeling under the blows from drunken or enraged adults, cringing in fear and dying on the inside from abusive words which define them as worthless and unlovable. Others dread hearing the approaching steps of one they know will abuse them sexually.

Adults feel they have fewer close friends than their parents had in past decades. Loneliness is a growing problem which too often results in alcoholism, drug abuse, physical abuse, suicide, depression, and sexual promiscuity.

What does all this mean? We must face the fact that America is in a state of moral collapse. We live in a country where there is a total breakdown of any standard of right or wrong.

I've not written this book just to complain and rehearse problems, but to expose the root cause of what is trying to destroy our great nation and sound a call to arms to the true sleeping giant in America — the Church of Jesus Christ. It is time for the Bride of Christ to wake up, put on the love and compassion of Jesus, strap on the power of the Holy Spirit, and hit the streets to take back what we have allowed the devil to steal from us: our people. As we deliver the message of the Gospel and set the captives of violence and hopelessness free, the world will witness a vibrant, powerful Church who is *Turning the Tide* in America!

# Chapter One

# Is America Lost?

Each day within the cities where you and I live unsuspected, senseless, and unprovoked crimes occur, seemingly unstoppable by limited police protection. We are having an eruption, an epidemic, of violence in our land. Drive-by shootings are happening, not in back alleys, but in the shopping malls on "Main Street."

Attorneys and judges, and the juries who are directed by them, have made the biggest mockery of justice in our history. One of the most frustrating jobs today is that of a police officer, who risks their life to arrest thugs who have beaten the brains out of other human beings — and then must watch a judge dismiss the cases. Law has become politically correct and justice is a joke!

Our schools are war zones. We can get into the airport easier than we can get into a local school, with their metal detectors and police roaming the halls. Gang members who were interviewed on television said they are often so bored on a Saturday night, they go out and shoot people just for the excitement.

This violence tells us there is no concept among our people that life has any value — no understanding of the sacredness and holiness of human life.

I don't know if you realize it, but many of the schools are teaching our seven-, eight-, and nine-year-olds a total disregard for human life — that it is compassionate to kill babies you don't want and get rid of the old folk who are no longer of any use.

A family I know were discussing their grandfather, who was very old and sick, and their young daughter overheard them. The child was raised in a Christian home and went to Sunday school, but from her public school she had found the solution to handling people who do not contribute to society. "We should kill Grandfather," she said, "because he is no longer bringing any money into the family. It's too hard to take care of him, so it would be a good thing for everyone if we were to kill him."

To add to this growing chaos, there is a total disregard for authority and what it means. Try to exert authority on this generation and you are met with a blank stare. The attitude is, "Who says? Just because you wear a blue uniform and a badge doesn't mean you can tell me what to do!"

Every school teacher has seen the lack of respect for authority from their students. But adults are no better. On the job, employees do not recognize the authority of the employer who pays them for their work.

On the home front, 30 percent of all births in America are outside of wedlock. Marriage is disregarded. We've reinvented it and called it "living together." Words like "commitment," "faithfulness," and "abstinence" are antiquated. We live with someone with no commitment, because it's convenient. We tell our partner, "Don't bank on tomorrow, because I can walk out whenever I want."

Moreover, there is a total confusion of the sexes. Some major Christian denominations are having to choose whether they will bless same-sex marriages. Before long, some of the biggest denominations in the country will be marrying and endorsing them.

It is ironic that with all this "freedom" going on, we are seeing unprecedented despair in our land. A hopelessness hangs over even our young. Obviously, something has gone very wrong. But what is it? Where did we get off the track?

## The Absence of Absolutes

Suddenly we're a society with no concept of responsibility for our actions; we no longer have a concept of sin or guilt. Those words are not in our vocabulary anymore. Therefore, we do not realize a standard has been broken and we are guilty because we broke it — because we do not recognize the existence of a standard in the first place.

In a recent poll, almost 40 percent of Americans said sometimes lying is necessary, and 67 percent said there is no such thing as absolute truth. Something may be true today, but not true tomorrow. In fact, 73 percent of mainline Protestant Christians do not believe in absolute truth. They do not believe the Ten Commandments are applicable to us today.

One "alleged" believer in four believes that Jesus made lots of mistakes and was not sinless, and 62 percent of unchurched people polled responded that the Church is not relevant today and has lost its influence upon society.

In any one of my audiences today, I would estimate that three out of ten do not believe adultery is wrong. Certainly, they don't believe lying is always wrong. It just depends on the circumstances.

Every night the television continually, subtly, blatantly — through movies, situation comedies, talk shows, and even the news — is coming across: "Having sex with anyone you want or beating your enemy to death with your fists is normal. You just have to grow up. The human race has come of age. Grow up!"

Media entertainment promotes programs about people who have no morals and live with anyone who happens to come along. You rarely see a marriage depicted. Instead, you watch as zillions of people hang out in bed together. But rarely do you see two people, particularly a man and a woman, committing themselves to each other for the rest of their lives.

Christians have said to me, "The idea that television and movies can actually change people's minds is ridiculous! Seeing adultery in a movie or on TV does not make you into an adulterer."

Why then, do advertisers pay millions of dollars for just a snippet between programs to influence people to buy their product? And you say television doesn't influence? The TV show has all evening to convince the viewer that the lifestyle they are portraying is normal.

"Adultery happens! Get with it, kid. You're faithful? How stupid. How dull. Look at how exciting adultery is! Do you want to miss out? You only live once, you know."

The creators and producers of these shows are the evangelists of humanism. Humanism enthrones the human being at the center of the universe instead of God. By doing this, we throw out all absolutes, because God is the only One who has any, and apart from God, we humans make up the rules as we go along.

We're brainwashed. Like ships tossed about in the blackness of a hurricane, we are spinning around and taking on water — and the captains have celebrated their personal freedom by throwing the compass overboard!

The Church is also on board this ship called Modern Civilization, but they are having a meeting down in the holds somewhere. They don't believe a captain could be so stupid as to throw the compass overboard, so they go merrily on, singing their hymns and having prayer rallies.

But prayer rallies alone won't solve this.

## No God — No Sin

In the last century America has thrown out law and moral absolutes. This is not to say that in the past all Americans kept the law and loved

God. But other generations at least knew the difference between right and wrong. This generation does not. We are humanistic; we're materialistic; we are the new pagan. We are as crooked, evil, and perverse as any generation has ever been in this country.

From an historical view alone, the judgment of God inevitably must come upon the humanism that has taken over America. Sin, which boils down to doing whatever we want to do instead of what God says to do, is the cancer of the universe, and if a society becomes so filled with this disease that they refuse to repent and turn back to God, there comes a time — God only knows when — when He must remove that cancerous society to avoid the destruction of the entire human race. We have seen this in history again and again.

There are civilizations who ruled the world whose names you have never heard. Only historians know they existed. Their inhabitants believed they would live forever, but today they're gone. They are buried in the sand or, like chaff, have been blown away by the winds of time. You can pay to see their ruins.... In some cases, even the race of that empire disappeared. Did you know there is not a living Roman on the planet today? Those who live in Italy are the conquerors of the Romans, not the Romans.

The demise of every great empire was marked by the same conditions: increase in homosexuality, abortion, and other immoral practices. These activities are the dying embers of a finished generation.

Just before Rome fell, life was so cheap that the government put on great circuses where Christians and others were killed for the afternoon entertainment. Tens of thousands would gather to watch people being torn to shreds by wild animals. Gladiators battled to the death. Today we have movies of such things, but in those days they did it live and in color.

*Human* life was cheap, but if they were cruel to an *animal,* they would be put to death. There were more protective laws for animals than for humans. Just before Rome fell, most Romans were vegetarians, because they would not eat animals.

Then the Goths and the Vandals came in and the Roman Empire began to fall apart. The Church was certain Jesus would be back any minute. They could not imagine a world without Rome, that 1500 years from where they stood, people would be paying to see the ruins of the Coliseum! It was impossible to think there would not be a living Roman on the face of the earth in just a few centuries, only the conquerors we now call Italians.

The lawlessness and immorality so many Americans are indulging in is exactly the same as what those fallen civilizations indulged in. And the darkness is much more intense than most believers are willing to admit. We have become a post-Christian nation.

At least atheistic primitives in Africa believe there is a world you cannot see and spirit powers in charge of what you can see. But many Americans do not even believe in the existence of a spirit world. We have gone so far from the truth, we do not believe anybody is in charge except ourselves.

We have thrown out God and all gods, and replaced them with a philosophy that exalts man. Because the Judeo-Christian God is unfashionable, we never hear the word "sin." In fact, it is politically incorrect to call someone a sinner. Instead, everyone has the right to pick their own lifestyle: You do your thing and I'll do mine. And we wonder why we have chaos on our hands!

Today when we mention the word "sin," even Christians get uncomfortable. Thus, we will never confront a person when they do something wrong. Did you know the correct way to describe a shoplifter is to call them an "alternate shopper"?

What has been the result of this mass abandonment of God and the concept of sin? In a hundred years of throwing out absolutes and the law, America has become a dysfunctional society, a people without any sense of meaning or purpose in life. Our cities are in a state of anarchy and collapse, our precious children are killing themselves, and our national debt is strangling us.

*The Bible would call us sheep who are lost.*

# Chapter Two

# What Does God Say?

Any objective observer could recognize that throwing out the Law of God has only destroyed American society. The love of God gave us the Law to produce a stable society with goals and ambitions, one that could bless the world. Take away that benevolent absolute, and society collapses. The Law of God was not given to make us miserable, but to teach us how to live, work, and play well together. It is not a list of "Do Nots" from a cruel taskmaster, but the grandest expression of God's love.

The words "unconditional love" speak of the love which is the very nature and essence of God. They express in English something of what the Greek word *agape* means. God is love, and the nature of His love is unlike human love in that He loves us because of who He is, not because of who we are.

Human love is created by the one we love. In other words, because someone is the kind of person they are or their performance is so very outstanding, they create in us what we call love. They draw it out of us. It is because of who they are that we feel about them the way we do. From here we get our expression, "fall in love." "Fall" is something we did not plan to do.

God never falls in love. He is not suddenly bowled over by the wonder of our great looks or exemplary behavior. He does not love us because of who we are or have been, or because we snowball Him with promises of what we are going to be.

Nor is God's love is ever to be thought of as His despising us in the state we are in now; putting up with us, knowing He will change us eventually to be the kind of person He could find loveable. He loves us now, just as we are, with all our faults and weaknesses. We can never earn the love of God. The love of God is bestowed freely upon us because *He is love*.

Unconditional love says we are loved even though we are doing what we are doing, but it does not stop there. God's love brings us back to the absolute. If there are no absolutes...and no sin...and no consequences...then what's so great about unconditional love?

Unconditional love loves us when we are wrong — and pursues us when we are wrong. *But it isn't soft on sin.* Because God is love and because He is good, He must, in His own time and wisdom, judge sin.

## Man's Rebellion

When God invented the universe, He set in order within it what we call laws. Science is the discovery of those laws. We may not like them, but we do not argue with them. We must submit to the laws within creation. Only then will they work for us.

A lesbian minister of a certain denomination has said that the Bible teaches that God made all things, and when He had finished, He said it was very good. "And," said she, "He made me, and I'm a lesbian, so I must be very good."

Wrong. After God made everything very *good*, mankind rejected God's order and everything became very *bad.* There was a *fall.* It is not a legend; it happened in time, space, and history. When the first couple went to the tree of the knowledge of good and evil, their feet made footprints in the mud.

Some of our mainline churches forget that what we see today is not the creation God made. This is the creation after the fall. And what happened afterward was different from what was before.

God gave one law to man in the Garden of Eden, a law intended to bring him to choose to become a fully mature human being, walking in submission to God. But man kicked over that law. He rebelled, declared himself independent, and stormed away from God's light and His love. He would make up his own meaning to life as he went along.

## The Final Absolute

Man was wrong — frighteningly and destructively wrong — but God's relentless unconditional love pursued him and gave him the Ten Commandments. As society broke these laws, society would destroy itself.

The Ten Commandments can be compared to the laws of physics. They are built into the way things are, just as the law of gravity is built into the very fabric of our universe. We could not stick to the planet without the law of gravity, and we cannot live full and meaningful lives without keeping the Ten Commandments.

The Ten Commandments told man how he was intended to live — in relationship with God, with others, and within himself. In them, God gave to mankind the blueprint, the owner's manual, for how to live life to the fullest.

The Ten Commandments comprise the very structure for being a normal human being. They are what makes a society healthy and happy. They give us the keys to how moral human beings function.

*The Law becomes to us a plumb line, the final absolute.*

Did you know it's the British who tell you what the time is? In London, on the River Thames, is a place called Greenwich. There, a clock sets the clocks of the entire world. So there is an absolute. We know when it is 10:30 in the morning — not because it feels like it ought to be, but because everybody on the planet agrees on Greenwich Mean Time.

How do we know how to live? Because the One who invented living is the absolute. By acknowledging Him and who He is, we can explain our universe and how we live in it. The Ten Commandments are set among us as the "Greenwich Mean Time" that tells us when we are "off." When we go against God's laws, we are completely off, as individuals and as a society.

Once man has suppressed the knowledge of the God who is his Creator, the source of his life, then he is left without an absolute. There's no "Greenwich Mean Time." He begins to explain life and try to understand its meaning with himself as the reference — and ultimately loses hope and purpose.

## Why Jesus Came

With all this talk of the law and the Ten Commandments, you would think Jesus Christ came to earth to enforce God's law. But He didn't. Salvation, our acceptance with God, has nothing to do with *our* keeping the law.

The fact is, we cannot keep it! Since the fall, we have an ingrained bent against God and His law. Every one of us has believed that, given enough time, we could bring to fruition the Lie that Satan told in the Garden: "Ye shall be as gods, knowing good and evil" (Genesis 3:5).

Our society has taken what happened in the Garden of Eden to its limit. We are our own gods, deciding from moment to moment what is good and what is evil. With the technology of today at our disposal, we have taken this concept around the world.

If we cannot keep the law, and salvation has nothing to do with our keeping the law, then we begin to see why Jesus came. He came to keep the law for us; He died on the cross to pay the debt for our sin or our inability to keep the law; and He was resurrected to offer us a new life.

Many confused people call themselves Christians, but they have not accepted Jesus Christ because their comprehension of Him and His demands is confused. They have never understood why He came and why He died. And the reason for that is, if they believe there are no absolutes and no sin, then why did He come in the first place? Why did He die? And why was He resurrected from the grave?

Luke 19:10 says He came "to seek and to save that which was lost." But if we do not have an absolute, then who's lost? If we do not have this absolute right at the center of our faith, then we just "sort of" accept Jesus. We walk to the front of the church, say a prayer we do not understand, sign a card, and get happy, but we don't know why He came or why we accepted Him. Our experience has no relationship to anything. It just feels good.

And we live in our world of no absolutes, return to church each week to sing about Jesus, but have no idea why we are doing it. Some never come back to church, believing all is now supposed to be okay.

## Understanding the Cross

The word we translate as "sin" means "to miss the mark." It is not like aiming at a bull's-eye and missing, but not even trying to hit the

17

bull's-eye. We set up an alternate target of our own, far away from God's absolute target.

If we choose to walk a path that "misses the mark," then we are rebels against God, which is eternally, deadly serious. Sin, if it had its way, would kill God. Remember, it began in the Garden with "I shall be as God."

Jesus took the unspeakable rebellion that all of us have been part of — a rebellion that involved aligning ourselves with Satan and deliberately disobeying God to go our own way — and bore it and all its consequences on the cross.

The only way for this rebellion to be dealt with was for Jesus to take our place. The sinless Son of God stands before the Father as us and for us, to receive the full, just punishment for the sins we have committed.

Salvation is recognizing Jesus' work on the cross — wiping out our debt of sin and freeing us from the shackles Satan had placed on us — and receiving His righteousness before God as a gift. His Holy Spirit comes to live within us, and our lives are transformed.

## God's Pursuing Love

Jesus tells the story of a sheep that was lost. To tell the parable in today's "religiously correct" language, we would say that the sheep had an alternative lifestyle from the rest of the flock. He probably came from a dysfunctional flock and thus could not be held responsible.

When Jesus said the sheep was lost, He was stating that the sheep's behavior was wrong! He was describing Himself as loving the sheep to the point that He would enter into its lostness in order to bring it back to order and life.

The very presence of Jesus Christ, the Son of God, in our history is a declaration that we are lost and that He came to do what we could not — to save us!

Behind the words "grace" and "mercy" is the fact that man has sinned, but God is not throwing him out with the garbage. He is coming after him to show him how wrong his actions are and how far from the norm he is.

Once the man recognizes his sin and lostness, God's unconditional love, manifested in the life, death, and resurrection of Jesus Christ, brings him not only to pardon and forgiveness, but back to the norm, to where he was created to be.

## Chapter Three

# Grace and Law

Jesus died, so we have been forgiven. Because of God's grace to us, the Law cannot condemn us. Does that mean God suspended His laws? Can we jump off the hundredth floor of a skyscraper and say, "It doesn't matter anymore. Jesus died, so there's no more law. Besides, God is a God of unconditional love. He wouldn't let us smash ourselves to bits on the pavement"?

No! Not only is the law of gravity still in effect, but so are the Ten Commandments — even though Jesus died and was resurrected. It is still sin to commit adultery, even though Jesus died for adulterers. It is still sin to steal, even though He was resurrected for thieves.

Some people believe that becoming a Christian means they can now do anything they please. Because they said the magic words and prayed the Sinner's Prayer, they now can become much more active sinners and God will keep on forgiving them.

That is nonsense! It reduces the Gospel to a fantasy, and it makes believers spiritual James Bonds with a "license to sin" — and the assured protection from all consequences.

God's unconditional love does not mean we are not responsible for our actions and we can now sin with no consequences. In Romans 6:1, Paul wrote about people who accused him of saying that any sin committed only showed the grace of God all the more. He posed the question: "Are we to continue in sin that grace might increase?"

Paul's response is one of the most violent in the New Testament: "May it never be!" You could almost see the man's face turning purple and ink spilling on the parchment. The very idea that the Gospel meant believers have diplomatic immunity and can now sin with no fear of consequences was blasphemy!

He addresses grace again in Titus 2:11 (NIV): "The grace of God that brings salvation has appeared to all men." Grace is simply unconditional love in action in our lives. What does grace do? It "...teaches us to say 'No' to ungodliness and worldly passions."

If the grace that has come into our life has not taught us to say no to sin, and if our understanding of grace is we can sin without any fear of consequences because God has suspended all moral law, then we totally misunderstand the Gospel.

When we say we are not under Law, that doesn't mean that, in our case, there are now no laws that apply — any more than we can stand on the edge of a cliff and say we are no longer under the law of gravity. We cannot jump off this cliff and not get hurt.

Jesus death and resurrection did not mean God scrapped the law. He came to fulfill the law Himself and then give us the means to be able to do the same.

## Man's Dignity

God created us with a dignity and an honor that places us far above the closest primate. Our dignity is that we are responsible to God in our actions. We are responsible to respond to the cross and to confess Jesus as Lord. We are responsible to walk with God, putting away sin. We still have the dignity of being human beings, but we are responsible to be true to the absolute.

The humanist has taken away man's dignity by saying he is not responsible for his actions. A government destroys the dignity of man by saying he does not have to work. He can just sit and be paid for being alive.

But we are human beings and that means we make choices. And when we choose to walk away from God's will and His presence in our lives, there are consequences. If God rules in love, He must judge those who perpetually oppose His love.

In that sense, God will not take away man's free will to save him from the consequences of his sin. Unconditional love is not saying that what we do does not matter. The path we have chosen will have consequences, but God will forever unconditionally love us in spite of those choices. Moreover, He will pursue us to the very end with His unconditional love.

Nevertheless, man must respond to the love of God, or he is spitting in the face of his only hope of salvation and placing himself under the wrath of God. To not accept Jesus Christ as Savior and Lord is to reject God's outstretched hand of unconditional love and forgiveness.

If we will go to hell, we must fight our way through the unconditional love of God — choosing to reject the cross and deny the power of the resurrection to get there. The reality of hell, however we would define or describe it, is the tragic monument to the reality of man's free will. It is, in fact, the fullest celebration of his free will and dignity. Ironically, the God he rejects is the One who gave him that dignity.

## Does God Stop Loving Us When We Sin?

If He did, that would mean He loved us in the first place because we were *not* sinning. And if God does not stop loving us when we sin, then why do we feel like He has deserted us when we do?

We have just realized we have a new nature on the inside of us, an absolute standard in our lives that opposes sin. When we do sin, we feel an immediate conviction of being wrong, of being guilty.

A lot of people who have made a wrong decision ask if it is possible to delete the bad consequences of their wrong actions. No, and that is our dignity. We sometimes wish we were something other than human beings, because we made a decision we can never reverse.

God cannot change consequences, but He can redeem them and cause them to become something we could never have dreamed of. He can create beauty from the ashes of our lives. The mercy of God works in consequences, if we repent and turn to His unconditional love and forgiveness.

In my own life, God has redeemed the dark holes, the blackest days. He not only forgave me and gave me a new life, but He redeemed those days. I understand the unconditionalness of His love, because I saw His grace and mercy toward me in spite of those black days. Now I have the rich soil in my life of unconditional love, grace, and mercy — only because of the black holes from whence I came.

Many people know they have broken God's law, and they try to honor it by admitting they have done wrong. These people return to the law of their resolutions and promises again and again; but along with the promises, they bring the guilt and shame from having broken the last promise they made.

It will always be this way, because the law cannot forgive, but only point to the wrong, the failure. There is always despair to the one who lives by the law, because the law can give no help to fulfill it, and the promises we make have no strength to bring them to fulfillment.

But in Jesus Christ's resurrection, ascension, and giving of the Holy Spirit, He imparts to us the power to achieve what He was always after — love. Furthermore, He pardons us, not by dismissing the law, but by fulfilling it for us.

The only way, then, that we can live is because grace pardons us. Grace gives us the opposite of what we deserve!

## The Spirit Within

Some would say that under the Old Covenant, people did not keep the law — the Ten Commandments — so, to God it was a total failure. The law didn't work, so we can throw it out and bring in something else. That is not what the Bible says.

God did not throw out the law by His grace. His grace relocated it into our hearts, which fulfilled the ancient prophecies.

Jeremiah 31:33 speaks of the New Covenant that would be made in Jesus, that in that day "I will put My law within them, and on their heart I will write it." And, "I will put My Spirit within you and cause you to walk in My statutes" (Ezekiel 36:27).

Ezekiel 11:19 said of the coming of the Lord Jesus, "I shall give them one heart, and shall put a new spirit within them...that they may walk in My statutes and keep My ordinances, and do them."

The Ten Commandments are no longer just an absolute "out there." They are within us, the Holy Spirit living in us. The plumb line has become our heart.

Therefore, we can now forget about the Ten Commandments, because we are keeping them! However, forgetting about them does not mean they are not there. We can forget about them because now they have been written in our hearts. They are not something imposed upon us; they are something inside us we love to fulfill.

The Holy Spirit who comes to live within us is separated from sin and begins the work of moving us away from sin. He was given not to make us feel good, but to grant us the power, the strength, and the ability to behave like Christ.

It takes a lifetime to accomplish this and to begin to produce in us the character of Christ that can be seen in our behavior. But, because the Spirit lives within us, when we do sin, we find there is hurt in our hearts. Red lights and alarm bells of conviction go off. He lets us know that this behavior we are now engaging in is not compatible with His living inside of us.

Immediately upon sinning, we recognize one more time that we are forgiven through what Jesus did. We know that by simply repenting — admitting our sin and turning from it back to Jesus — the red lights and alarm bells will stop and peace will return to our hearts.

## Chapter Four

# An Awful Void to Fill

God's love has come. There is no more doubt, no more searching in the darkness. We know the love of God, when He himself took the sins of those who would rebel against Him. He took our judgment in Jesus. He bore our griefs, our sorrows, our sins, and He carried them away.

Whether or not we have broken the Ten Commandments is no longer the issue. No man is lost today because he breaks the Ten Commandments, because Jesus has paid the penalty of sin (1 John 5:12).

John 16:8,9 says the Holy Spirit "will convict the world concerning sin...because," said Jesus, "they do not believe in Me." This does not say He will convict the world because they have broken the Ten Commandments, but because they will not receive Jesus as their Savior and Lord and thus be pardoned from their sin. Upon receiving Jesus, the Holy Spirit comes to live in them and begin the process of making them holy.

So the issue is, will we receive Jesus Christ's pardon? Will we submit to salvation in Him? If not, there is nowhere else to turn and nothing else to wait for.

Scripture says man has rebelled not only against God and the Ten Commandments, but against God in His coming to us in Jesus. Many men have refused to submit to that salvation.

That is why Scripture says, "This is the condemnation, that light is come into the world, and men loved darkness rather than light, because their deeds were evil" (John 3:19 KJV). When the Light came, man fled to the darkness like a bug back to its basement.

Man was made for God, and there is a vacuum in him that can only be filled with the infinite God — a craving for love that can only be filled by His unconditional love.

If man refuses that Light, deliberately turning his back upon God and the offered pardon, seeking to find his own unconditional love and fill the vacuum in his own way — then there is an awful void in him.

Man can then only begin to fill the void with his own ideas of meaning and significance — and they are all destructive.

## God Substitutes

The person who substitutes money for God seeks to fill that void with wealth. At first it is fun, but eventually he will destroy himself with greed and certainly destroy his family.

The person who uses drugs or alcohol as means of escape from the pain of that emptiness within eventually destroys himself — and the society that does not deal with the problem.

Homosexuality is nothing more than a craving for unconditional love that is searching in all the wrong places. This is so destructive to society that it is not a private matter.

One of our government leaders has said there is nothing in the Ten Commandments about homosexuality. This only shows they are biblically illiterate. Throughout the books of Leviticus, Deuteronomy, and Numbers, the Ten Commandments are explained and expanded upon, and certain things are considered the ultimate evil acts, called the abominations. Homosexuality is one of those abominations.

People often ask me why God is against homosexuality. Why is He against adultery, murder, or stealing? If stealing is legal, we can kiss goodbye to our property. If adultery is right, we will soon see the end of the family. Homosexuality, according to Scripture, is an abomination which will destroy society. If we do not believe the Bible, look at the empires that all went the same way we are going and ended...with a celebration of homosexuality.

Don't misunderstand me. I am not carrying banners over homosexuals to damn them to hell. The practicing homosexual needs to know God loves them and is not afraid of them. He loves lesbians. God never stops loving us. We are the ones who run away from Him.

God gave me His love for these people. I totally love and accept them as human beings for whom Jesus Christ has died. But I hate homosexuality, as I do all sin. The fact is, the Bible makes it abundantly clear — back to the absolute — that this is sin. If people continue in a lifestyle of sin, they set themselves in a posture of being enemies of God.

I do not tell the homosexual that, because God loves them, they can carry on in that lifestyle. Rather, because God loves them, for His sake, they should turn around and receive His love, and let Him make them whole.

God says the abortionist cannot murder. And I am totally opposed to the fanatics who blow away abortion doctors. The moment they murder or attempt to murder an abortion doctor, they have done nothing less than join the ranks of the murdering abortionists.

The abortion doctor, or anyone who has aborted a child, needs to know God loves them with an unconditional love. Jesus has already borne the sin of murder, but they must receive His pardon.

One of the most beautiful testimonies I ever heard about the abortion issue was from a grandmother who wrote a letter to an abortion doctor. She said:

"I'm writing to say I forgive you because you were paid, sort of as a hit man, to be the murderer of my grandchild. I never saw my grandchild, because you murdered him. But I forgive you, and I am praying for you, and I want you to know that God loves you. My hope is that I shall see my grandchild in heaven."

The doctor said this was the first Christian who ever indicated to him that he was loved. That letter led him eventually to Christ.

People say, "But I want to leap from bed to bed and have as many babies as I choose, or trash them if I don't want them." That destroys society. If we can kill babies, then why can't we kill them after they are born? What's the difference? They have a beating heart; they are alive.

God speaks of the woman, from the moment of conception, as being "with child." Psalm 139 says God weaves every part of that child in the womb. He does not say it is a piece of tissue. It is a living child, a human being.

If we can kill that child because it is a burden to us, then why not kill anyone else who is a burden? This child is stopping us from having fun! Trash the kid!

If you keep up with the news, you know I am just quoting headlines. When we trash babies, we introduce into society an evil spirit of violence that dispenses with everyone who gets in our way, that looks upon blowing people away as fun to be had on a Saturday night.

## What Has Happened to the Church?

It is a solemn thing to live at this point in time in America. To speak of coming judgment is foolishness. We are in the midst of judgment! That is why the headlines read as they do and our government has the corruption it has.

We're free! Then, why aren't we dancing? We've never had such a generation of despair, disgust — so many bored people, confused, filled with anxiety and dread, a terrifying dread of tomorrow.

We're like the dog that finally caught the car. The world has gone sour and stale. And this has happened before...happened again and again, actually. In every case, if history teaches us anything, we know it has led to divine surgery, the judgment of God.

Out of the ruins and rubble there arises a wiser, humbler people who start the cycle all over again — and end up down the road doing the same things.

But let me give you some hope, because with such a study as we have here, you could spiral into despair very quickly! The nearest our generation can get in biblical model would be Sodom and Gomorrah. And God said He would spare the city if He could find enough righteous.

I do not write this book just to say how bad civilization is. I write it with the hope that the Church will wake up and be the Church. We could be the grandest shining forth of the Light.

I remember as a little boy listening to Winston Churchill on radio, telling us to fight in the streets and on the beaches. Even though I was so young, I remember him saying, "Britain, this is your finest hour!"

And I say, Church, in this bottom of the cesspool in which we find ourselves, this is not a time to give up. This is your finest hour. Be who you are in the Holy Spirit!

## A Gospel to Live For

I believe one of the reasons the Church is so impotent in the face of our humanistic culture is because we have been taught that coming to Jesus Christ has only to do with after death or after the end of time.

We have taught people that to come to Christ is to get ready to die — to get ready for the rapture. In meeting after meeting where I preach, inevitably an appeal is given for persons to become Christians — which is fine. I have no problem with that. But I would say at least 60 to 80 percent of those appeals made are based on life after death. They go something like this:

"If you died tonight, where would you spend eternity? Are you ready to face Jesus?" And variations on that theme.

Therefore, we find ourselves waiting until we die so we can be with Jesus. We just hang out, with nothing to say and nothing to show to the culture in which we live. We have had our brains turned to "after death."

The New Testament knows nothing of that. There is not one reference to be found that anybody ever invited anybody else to come to

Christ in order to be ready to die. They came to Christ to be ready to live!

The Church must return to the understanding that salvation means a change in behavior. The whole New Testament's burden is that in this here and now you will stop doing *that* and you will take up *this*.

Then the grace of God, the Spirit of Jesus Christ freely given to live the life of Christ through us, enables us to live such a lifestyle.

If we get it into our heads that coming to Jesus Christ is something to do with being okay after we die, then what has it to do with living in our homes or working in our office? What does it have to do with our school? Absolutely nothing.

## Christianity Is Not Magic

Christianity is not saying a prayer just so we go to heaven. Christianity is death to the world. It is a total, radical, different way of looking at and living life. It is repenting and saying that every way we looked at life and everything we built our life upon was wrong.

We receive God's pardon, forgiveness, and the living Spirit of Jesus Christ to come live in us and produce a whole new lifestyle. We have a new understanding of ourself and of others. We treat people differently. Our expectancies of tomorrow are different. We have hope instead of despair.

Our outlook on life will never be the same, in our marriage, our home, where we work, our place as a citizen. Everything changes because we have seen the truth as it is in Jesus. We learn how to have Christ himself as the very energy of our life.

## Chapter Five

# The Church's Response

How does the Church respond to the darkness of a humanistic society? How do we live as lights that shine in the darkness?

The Church must come to understand that to be a Christian is a matter of behavior. It is Christ living in us — His strength and love and our choosing to live by them. We must:

## 1. Pray Without Ceasing

James 4:2 says, "You do not have because you do not ask." The Church must learn how to ask of God. The key word to prayer is asking. You cannot pray without asking.

There are many believers who have never really asked for anything in the name of Jesus. Why not? Because unbelief makes them afraid to ask. Unbelief is scared to put God on the spot by asking, so it retreats back into traditional pious religious language.

Some have come from religious backgrounds that bound them with rituals and do's and don'ts that are void of the Living God. They were taught never to ask, so they squashed the very possibility of ever wanting anything from God enough to ask Him.

If you have come from such a background, then the idea of asking and expecting to receive something back from God is totally foreign. Let me announce to you, you are no longer involved in religion. You have come to the Living God, you are in Christ, and it is now okay to ask. You have come to a God who has the resources. He loves you and wants to give to you. He says if you will only ask, He will give.

Prayer, as defined in the New Testament, is the focus of the supernatural nature of Christianity. This is where we prove, and we live in the fact, that our Father is alive, He loves us, and Jesus really did walk this planet. He did die, rise, is alive, and has sent the Holy Spirit.

But that is where many back off. They don't want to be disappointed. Maybe they don't believe what they said they believed. So they will not ask anything of God, and then they won't have to put Him to the test.

We must renew our minds with God's Word in order to believe. We must bring our lives and our minds into line with what we have now discovered in Christ. We must repent of the religion that has paralyzed us for so long — and has forbidden us to ask plainly and simply of our Father.

Prayer is the going forth of our spirit. We are engaged upon the highest order of creature-hood. We are talking to the Creator. He who comes to God must believe that He is there, that He is the communicating God, and that we are the communicating human. We are coming together to talk.

It is no small thing to ask of God. You look upon a suffering world, a brokenhearted neighbor, a sick family member, a family being ripped to pieces with divorce, or a teenager who is full of drug problems, and there rises in you a holy anger, born of the Spirit. Look at what the devil has done!

Your love for those people reaches to them and you say, "In the name of the Lord Jesus Christ, Who died for these people, Who is risen, Who redeemed them from such a terrible condition — in His name I say it shall not be so." Out of that, you ask of Father.

It is not a whim. It is not just a wish. It is your will put into your words. It is asking for what you want. Therefore, it is focused.

Furthermore, the length of a prayer list is not important; it is not how much you pray for, but what you pray for. It would be better to visit with God for an afternoon so you can focus on what you are really asking for, than to go through a long list of things when you don't really know what you are asking for.

When God tells us to ask what we wish, He is seeking to draw us out. He is forever trying to bring us to the full potential of who we are. The New Testament teaches that it is God's will for us to ask of Him, for prayer is where we discover what faith really is.

I worked with drug addicts, hippies, and prostitutes in New York City for a number of years before I began traveling. As they came to Jesus Christ, they put me to shame for their simplicity, because they had never read all the theology books. They hadn't been exposed to religion with all its doubt-filled questions.

When they came, straight off the streets of New York City, and they read what the Bible said, they did it! And it worked!

I have seen hippies and prostitutes, born again in the morning, praying for the sick in the evening and seeing the sick healed — while people who have been in the church for years still have not found the faith inside to pray for anything!

We must repent of a lot of religion and become like little children, believing when we don't understand. We can talk about humility and surrendering to God, but it actually happens when we ask, because asking is acknowledging our helplessness.

To handle life in the love of God, in His wisdom, we surrender to Him — and in asking, we experience submission. The only way we know how to surrender is to ask Father to come. Then by us, through us, and for us, He will give the wisdom, the ability, and if necessary, work the miracles.

Asking is where faith comes into action. Prayer is a commitment. It is abandonment. You are not trying it out to see if it works. The kind of faith we admire whenever we see it only happens in the arena of asking. Up until then, it is theory, books, and sermons. The rubber hits the road when you ask.

Ask! Begin to think of your whole life as a partnership with God the Creator, your Father. You walk through life and you are never alone. As needs are presented to you, ask and you will receive.

Learn to join your will to the will of God. There is no greater power on the face of this planet than your will submitted and joined to the will of God. And out of that will, when you ask of Father and you receive, you will shape and change your world.

## 2. Pray for the Church

We have a tent meeting mentality, so that every time we come together we must preach the Gospel and try to get people to become Christians. Every time we pray, we must pray for all the unsaved.

We say, "Put up your hand. Walk forward. Shake the pastor's hand. Sign this card. Say the Sinner's Prayer." Where is any of that in the New Testament?

*In the last hundred years, we have reinvented how to become Christians, because all that I have just mentioned is not in the Bible.*

In the Bible, you confess Jesus Christ is Lord. Nowhere in Scripture do you walk forward and say a prayer. The adequate response to the Gospel is Acts 2:38: "Repent, and let each of you be baptized in the name of Jesus Christ for the forgiveness of your sins; and you shall receive the gift of the Holy Spirit."

When we return to the model of the New Testament Church that stood in the darkness, they came together and prayed for themselves. The strong Church knows who they are and is exhibiting the energy of the life of the risen Jesus. The strong Church will draw the outsider to it.

When the outsider comes in, he will behold a behavior and a lifestyle from which he can learn how to live, from those who are already living from the life of Christ.

I believe in praying for the unsaved, but the Church prays for believers, because if the believers are who they are meant by God to be, then the unconverted are going to come.

If we can become who we are in Christ, if our eyes can be opened, if our inner selves can be strengthened, if we can know the energy of the Holy Spirit so that we increase in spiritual wisdom and understanding and have a lifestyle that is pleasing to God, then we will be the light of the world.

# 3. Change Our View of Christian Initiation

If the Church is going to stand in the midst of a humanistic world, we must have a radical change of outlook in terms of initiation, in bringing others to Christ.

To become a Christian in the earliest days was not so easy as it is today. Maybe we make it too easy. Maybe we are so desperate to have numbers that we shortchange people.

Our churches are filled with people who don't even know who Jesus Christ is and they think they're saved, because no one ever spoke to the humanistic philosophy they had when they came in. They are trying to build truth on a foundation of lies.

In the early Church, when persons turned up saying they wanted Christ, they didn't come in immediately. Believers would sit down and confront them with truth. They would take a long time explaining that this is a conversion — a total turning of our lifestyle on its head. After coming into Christ, they would not be living the way they had been. They would not have the behavior they had in the past.

They would point out areas of their lifestyle that were going to change. And they were not told they had to change in their own strength, but in God's. They were to understand that the Holy Spirit was going to change them. He would redeem them to a whole new person.

In today's world, the man on the street does not know who Jesus Christ is. He has no concept of a God who is personal, infinite, triune, and the meaning of our life today. The time is long over when we can just say, "Come to Jesus," because nobody knows who He is.

Our coming to God depends on our confessing that Jesus is the Son of God, says 1 John 4:15. It means we understand He is Lord because He's risen from the dead. And He's risen from the dead because He died. And He died because He came. And He came via the womb of the Virgin Mary, and He is the eternal Son of God who came.

The man on the street and the drifter in your church don't know that. And when we proclaim the Gospel, we must proclaim the whole counsel of God. And maybe not all at one time.

There is such a panic to get people to say the magic words of the Sinner's Prayer, in case they should die on the way home, that we do them eternal, grave harm. Read the Acts of the Apostles. Paul debated with people, discussed with them, argued with them. He presented his case: The truth against their lies.

There was no panic, no telling them to receive a Jesus they did not even know. He wanted them to understand God the Father Who created all things, that they were made by God, with a responsibility to Him that was built into them as human beings.

We don't repent with a blink, because to repent means a radical change of mind. We must face up to sin, understand what it is, understand where we have been distorted in our thinking, and now turn from that.

## 4. Have A Radical Reevaluation of Our Evangelism

Seventy years ago you could just say to a person, "Come to Jesus," because every American knew who Jesus was. When I came to America in 1964, everybody knew what the Gospel was. If they didn't accept it, they knew what they weren't accepting.

Today, nobody knows. We must start from square one. We have to start in the unbeliever's despair. We must address it with the Gospel and bring them to the incredible love God has for a rebellious person.

The persons who come into our churches come in with invisible chains of darkness. We can't just have them "say this prayer after me." Those chains are broken by truth — by prayer.

We are talking about a nation that is demonized. This wasn't so when I first came over here. I have met the demonic powers in Africa, the Philippines, and China, and I have begun to see the same demonic activity in the United States. Things I thought belonged in Africa now are at home in America. The demons that once lived elsewhere live here now.

We live in a demonized society, because once we have put God out of His heaven in our minds, we have to fill it with something else. And because man is an incorrigibly religious person, he has filled his mind with the demonic, the "New Age," and neo-paganism.

At school our teenagers are not only surrounded by the philosophy of humanism, but by the symbolism of Satan, with gangs who wear the pentagram. What has the Church given them? How do we tell them to face that?

"Oh, pray about it. Plead the blood."

The early Church gave them something so powerful that they knew they were no longer of that world. They had passed through baptism, and they now stood clothed in Christ, one with the Body of Christ on earth. They knew they were in and why.

Many areas of the Church have driven their teenagers away because they have confused local custom with divine absolutes. The teens were told they couldn't do this, they couldn't do that, they mustn't go there — while their parents indulged in bitterness, malicious gossip, lying, and cheating on their income tax — breaking divine absolutes while imposing silly local customs on their children.

Our teenagers are crying out. They are screaming for some sense to a despairing world that is leading them to suicide. In church after church, we treat our teenagers as we did seventy years ago. Yet, they know more today than we knew when we were forty! They don't want little church programs. They want to know the answer to life! They want to know the answer to despair. They want to know how to stand up against satanism. They want a framework in which to understand the meaning of existence.

That's evangelism.

I put it to some of you parents: Don't think that just because your children go off to a happy little youth meeting everything is okay. You had better find out what is being taught at that youth meeting, because your kids have questions that perhaps your local church does not even know, let alone the answers for them.

You had better have some serious talks with your teens about the meaning of life and the despair that might be taught to them in school, the hopelessness that could be being drummed into their heads.

## 5. Be Baptized

The early Church took baptism very seriously. Recognizing that their sins had been placed upon Christ, they would come to baptism with a three-fold statement: We renounce the world, its whole philosophy, that craving to be independent of God and "do my thing." We renounce the flesh and submit to Jesus Christ. And we renounce the devil and all his works.

This was no quick decision. This was something you came to intelligently, and it was hedged by repentance and faith.

## 6. Go Into the World

Jesus said to go into the world and preach the Gospel. Obviously, He meant all the nations of the world, but maybe there is a deeper meaning there.

You go into *your world.* If you happen to be an attorney, go into your world of attorneys. I am no use there. Attorneys have buzz words; they have their lingo.

Go into your world of the factory, into your world of medical doctors, into your world of secretaries, into your world of high school, into your world — whatever your world is — from the community of light where Christ is your life. Go into the world and hold out the Gospel.

You are going with a behavior that tells it all. You don't have to work at the way you live. If you know the Gospel and begin to live in accord with it, you will stand out like the light that you are in a world of impersonal despair.

Over against the canvas of how you are living, you are ready to give an answer for the hope which is within you. You are ready to make contact with people who are in despair. You penetrate your world as a believer.

And when people are ready to hear, you are ready to talk and share where you are coming from.

## 7. Share the Covenant Meal

I have made a study of the early Church — not the one in the Bible, but the one that started at the end of the New Testament. The one that was persecuted and beaten, thrown to the lions, and beheaded and burned at the stake. And yet, they came out triumphant.

What was their secret? There was one thing they did every week, sometimes every day, even when they were waiting in those chambers about to be thrown to the lions. In a moment, the doors would be opened and they would be pushed out into the arena to meet the wild animals. What did they do just before they went out? They shared the Covenant Meal, Holy Communion.

The early Church recognized there had to be one time when they were not evangelizing; when they were not doing, they were taking.

The wild animals were baying out there. They could hear the snarls and the roars of leopards and lions and tigers waiting for them. Yet they knelt around a simple table and ate bread and drank wine and glorified Jesus. Then they went out singing songs of praise to God. They were strengthened. They had met with the Living Jesus. They had a center.

They gathered in the tunnels that ran under Rome, in old warehouses, and out in graveyards where Romans were afraid to go. Fearing persecution, they met before dawn, kneeling and worshiping the Lamb who sits upon the throne.

If you do that every week, your whole life begins to be brought into divine order.

## In Summary

In this time, at the end of the 20th century, we are not going to make it unless we are plugged in to the Body of Christ. And unless that Body reexamines its initiation process, stops its insane thrashing and frenzy of activity, and learns to meet with the Living Christ at the Holy Communion table, we're not going to make it.

We have gone the full cycle and are back in the darkness of first century of humanism. We need a working Church, as it worked in the first centuries, or we are not going to make it. We will go down with the ship. We need a true Church in every city.

This humanistic world, which is already burned out on its emptiness, weary with going around in pointless circles, will gravitate toward people who are living sanely — and people who are not screaming at them that they are sinners. We are the living Body of Christ, exposing the Gospel by our behavior.

We must understand that we are the light of the world, that light is behavior, and that light shines. It penetrates into the darkness of a confused, weary, and crazed society.

We, the Church, are a community; we are not individualistic. The New Testament never sees one isolated believer out in the world alone, with God doing all His fantastic work in them. The light shines when we are joined to other believers and we love one another in that fellowship of believers. Together, we shine out into the world.

Wherever we find ourselves, in whatever group of believers He joins us to, that is where we work out our Christianity, where we are the light of the world, where we understand the Gospel and pass it on.

# Endnotes

Statistics in the Preface and Chapters One and Two were taken from:

*1993 George Barna Seminar on Understanding Ministry in a Changing Culture*, Barna Research Group, LTD.

*The Frog in the Kettle: What Christians Need to Know About Life in the Year 2000*, by George Barna, Regal Books, a division of Gospel Light, Ventura, CA 93006, 1990.

*Ministry Currents*, Vol.II, Number 4, by Barna Research Group, LTD, 647 West Broadway, Glendale, CA 91204, October-December 1992.

# Other Books
# by Malcolm Smith:

*Spiritual Burnout*

*The Unconditional Love Series:*

*Toxic Love: The Illusion of Self-Worth*

*Forgiveness*

*No Longer A Victim*

*Let God Love You*

*The Healing Heart of God*

*Never Lonely Again*

For a complete list of books and tapes:

Malcolm Smith Ministries

P. O. Box 29747

San Antonio, TX 78229-0747

210-614-3838